play
bass
today!

by Chris Kringel
Recorded at Beat House, Milwaukee, Wisconsin

ISBN 978-0-634-06236-0

HAL•LEONARD®
CORPORATION
7777 W. BLUEMOUND RD. P.O. BOX 13819 MILWAUKEE, WI 53213

Visit Hal Leonard Online at
www.halleonard.com

Introduction

Track 1

Welcome to *Play Bass Today!*—the series designed to prepare you for any style of bass playing, from rock to blues to jazz to country. Whatever your taste in music, *Play Bass Today!* will give you the start you need.

About the CD

It's easy and fun to play bass, and the accompanying CD will make your learning even more enjoyable, as we take you step by step through each lesson and play each song along with a full band. Much like with a real lesson, the best way to learn this material is to read and practice a while first on your own, then listen to the CD. With *Play Bass Today!*, you can learn at your own pace. If there is ever something that you don't quite understand the first time through, go back on the CD and listen again. Every musical track has been given a track number, so if you want to practice a song again, you can find it right away.

Contents

The Basics

Track 2

The Parts of the Bass

The bass is a great instrument—it holds down the bottom of the band, and it's easy and fun to play.

Although there are many different kinds of basses—including models with five, six, and even seven strings—the typical bass has four strings and all the parts shown to the right. Take some time to get acquainted with the parts of your bass.

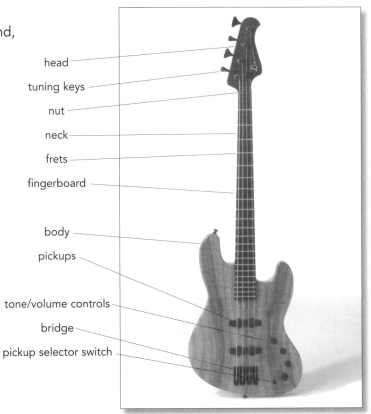

head

tuning keys

nut

neck

frets

fingerboard

body

pickups

tone/volume controls

bridge

pickup selector switch

How to Hold Your Bass

Sitting is probably the easiest position when first learning to play. Rest the bass on your right thigh and hold it against the right side of your chest, keeping your feet flat on the floor—or rest the bass on your left thigh and hold it against the center of your chest and slightly elevate your left leg. If you have a strap, you may prefer to stand. It is a good idea to start with a strap to find the most comfortable position for your bass.

The height and balance of your bass should be the same standing or sitting. Find a position that is comfortable for you—whatever position you choose, your hands must be free to move across the strings. Therefore, don't hold the bass with your hands; support it with your body or with a strap.

Your Right and Left Hands

You'll be playing your bass by plucking the strings with your right hand—using either your fingers or a pick. To play with your fingers, find a place to rest your thumb. Use your index and middle fingers to pluck the strings with an upward motion (toward your chest). To play with a pick, grip it between the thumb and index finger, keeping the rest of your hand relaxed and your fingers curved, and strike the strings in a downward motion. The fingers not holding the pick may rest on the bass for extra support.

Your left hand belongs on the neck of the bass. It, too, should be relaxed. To help you get a feel for the correct hand placement, follow these suggestions:

1. Place your thumb on the underside of the neck, positioned in the middle.

2. Arch your fingers so that you will be able to reach all the strings more easily.

3. Avoid letting the palm of your hand touch the neck of the bass.

Playing Is Easy

If you haven't already, try plucking the strings of your bass. Notice that some strings sound higher and some sound lower? Each has a different *pitch*. Pitch is the highness or lowness of a sound. On the bass, the strings are numbered 1 through 4, from the highest-sounding string (the thinnest) to the lowest-sounding one (the thickest).

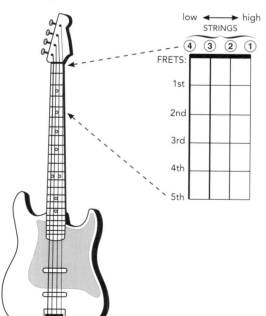

You get different pitches from each bass string by pressing it down on various frets with the fingers of your left hand. Fretting higher up the neck produces sounds of a higher pitch; fretting lower on the neck produces sounds of a lower pitch. As you can see, the frets of the bass are also numbered, from low (near the head) to high (near the body).

The fingers of your left hand will also be numbered in this book, for convenience:

Tuning Up

If you loosen a string by turning its tuning key, the pitch will become lower; if you tighten the string, the pitch will become higher. When two pitches sound exactly the same, they are said to be *in tune*. There are many ways to get your bass in tune: you may use an electronic tuner, a piano, a pitch pipe, a tuning fork—you can even tune your bass purely to itself. For now, however, listen to the audio to help you tune your instrument. The bass's four open strings should be tuned to these pitches:

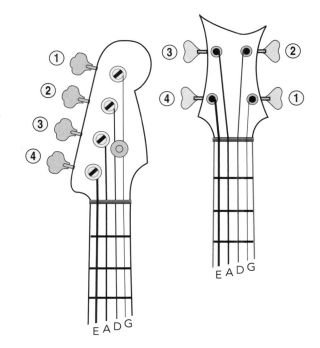

④ ③ ② ①
E–A–D–G
low ⟵⟶ high

Here are a few tips to help get you started:

- Whether tightening or loosening a string, turn the peg slowly so that you can concentrate on the changes in pitch. You may need to pick the string repeatedly to compare it.

- As you're tuning a string, you may notice that a series of pulsating **beat waves** becomes audible. These beat waves can actually help you tune: they'll slow down as you get closer to bringing two pitches together, and they'll stop completely once the two pitches are exactly the same.

- Instead of tuning a string *down* to pitch, tune it *up*. Tuning up allows you to stretch the string into place, which will help it stay in tune longer. So, if you begin with a string that is too high in pitch, tune it down first, and then bring it back up to pitch.

Another Way to Tune Your Bass

This is a great way to check your tuning or, if you don't have a pitch source like the CD, to tune you bass to itself.

1. Tune the 4th string E to a piano, a pitch pipe, an electronic tuner, or the CD. If none of these are available, approximate E the best you can.

2. Press the 4th string at the 5th fret. This is A. Tune the open 3rd string to this pitch.

3. Press the 3rd string at the 5th fret. This is D. Tune the open 2nd string to this pitch.

4. Press the 2nd string at the 5th fret. This is G. Tune the open 1st string to this pitch.

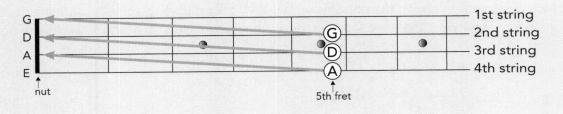

How to Read Music

Musical sounds are indicated by symbols called **notes**. Notes come in all shapes and sizes, but every note has two important components: pitch and rhythm.

Pitch

Pitch (the highness or lowness of a note) is indicated by the placement of the note on a **staff**, a set of five lines and four spaces. Notes higher on the staff are higher in pitch; notes lower on the staff are lower in pitch.

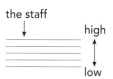

To name the notes on the staff, we use the first seven letters of the alphabet: **A–B–C–D–E–F–G**. Adding a **bass clef** assigns a particular note name to each line and space on the staff, centered on the pitch F, the fourth line from the bottom. In the bass clef, in which most music for the electric bass is written, the names of the lines, starting with the first line, are G, B, D, F, and A. The names of the spaces, starting with the first space, are A, C, E, and G.

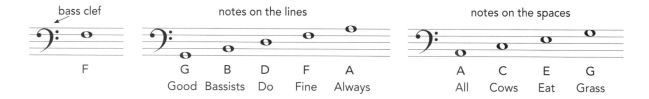

Rhythm

Rhythm refers to how long, or for how many beats, a note lasts. This is indicated with the following symbols:

whole note
(four beats)

half note
(two beats)

quarter note
(one beat)

To help you keep track of the beats in a piece of music, the staff is divided into **measures** (or "bars"). A **time signature** (or "meter") at the beginning of the staff indicates how many beats you can expect to find in each measure.

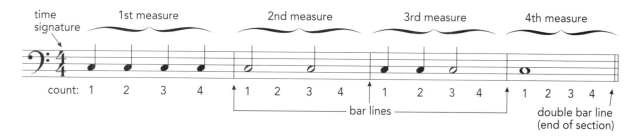

4/4 is perhaps the most common time signature. The top number ("4") tells you how many beats there are in each measure; the bottom number ("4") tells you what type of note value receives one beat. In 4/4 time, there are four beats in each measure, and each beat is worth one quarter note.

Intervals

The smallest distance, or interval, between two notes is called a **half step**. If you play any note on the bass and then play another note one fret higher or lower, you have just played a half step. If you move two frets higher (two half steps up) or two frets lower (two half steps down), you have moved one **whole step**.

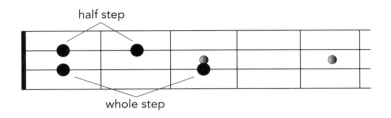

Accidentals

Any note can be raised or lowered a half step by placing an **accidental** directly before it.

Sharp (♯)   ⟶   Raises a note one half step (one fret)

Flat (♭)   ⟶   Lowers a note one half step (one fret)

Natural (♮) ⟶ Cancels previously used sharp or flat

Ledger Lines

Notes higher or lower than the range of the staff must be written using **ledger lines**. Ledger lines can be used above or below the staff.

The First String: G

The first three notes we'll learn on the bass are all found on the highest (and thinnest) string. This is the first string, also called the G string.

G

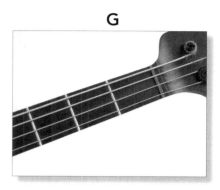

■ Your first note, G, is an "open-string" tone. There's nothing to fret—simply pluck the open first string.

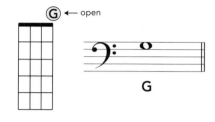

A

► Notice that your finger actually belongs *directly behind* each metal fret. If you place it on top of the fret, or too far back, you'll have difficulty getting a full, clear sound.

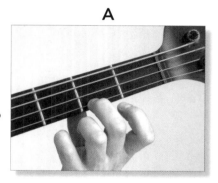

■ For the next note A, place your second finger on the second fret, and pluck the string.

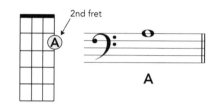

B

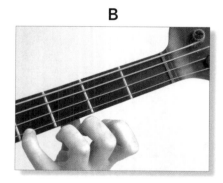

■ To play the note B, place your fourth finger on the fourth fret, and pluck the string.

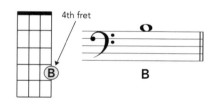

Learn to recognize these notes both on the fretboard *and* on the staff. Then, when you're comfortable playing the notes individually, try this short exercise. Speak the note names aloud as you play (e.g., "G, A, B, A...").

G-A-B

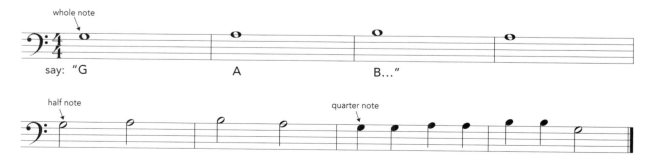

Of course, the best way to really learn these notes is to use them in some tunes. So let's do it. Start slowly with the following melodies, and keep your pace nice and even.

First Song

Track 6

Keeping Time

Having trouble keeping a steady rhythm? Try *tapping* and *counting* along with each song. If the bass is resting on your right leg, use your left foot to tap. Each time the foot comes down marks one beat. In 4/4 time, tap your foot four times in each measure, and count "1, 2, 3, 4." The first beat of each measure should be accented slightly—this is indicated below by the symbol ">."

count and tap: 1   2   3   4   1   2   3   4   1   2   3   4   1   2   3   4

Second Song

Track 7

▶ If you like, read through each song *without* your bass first: Tap the beat with your foot, count out loud, and *clap* through the rhythms.

Third Song

Track 8

Two New Notes: G♯ and B♭

Notice that we skipped the first and third frets? Let's go back and grab those notes.

G♯

▶ Remember sharps (♯) and flats (♭)? If not, review page 7.

■ To play the note G♯, place your first finger on the first fret.

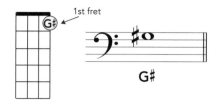

B♭

■ To play the note B♭, place your third finger on the third fret.

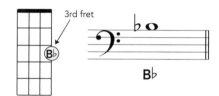

Let's try these new notes in a song.

Track 9

▶ Sharps and flats apply throughout the measure in which they appear.

G♯-B♭

Track 10

Play It!

Now here are some tunes to practice all five notes you've learned so far. Don't be afraid to review G, A, and B again before tackling these!

Track 11

▶ Remember: A natural sign (♮) cancels a previous sharp or flat.

Mix It Up

Mix It Down

Track 12

Track 13

Technique

Now we'll take a look at our left and right hand positions.

The Left Hand

Be sure to keep your left hand fingers curved but relaxed, and use just your fingertips to fret the notes. In this next exercise, try to keep your fingers down when you are finished fretting a note; when you are done, all your fingers should be touching the first string. Place your thumb on the back of the neck adjacent to your second finger. Keep your touch light.

The Right Hand

If you're using your fingers to pluck the strings, alternate back and forth: index then middle. Keep your fingers close to

the string so you are able to strike the string cleanly and precisely. If you're using a

pick, strike the strings with a downward motion—remember, you are only going to play with the point of the pick, not the body.

The Second String: D

Track 14

Your next three notes are all played on the second string, D. You might want to check your tuning on that string before going any further.

D

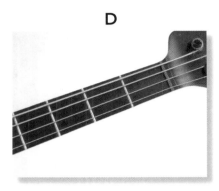

■ To play the note D, just pluck the open second string.

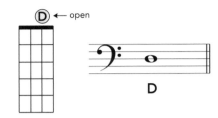

E

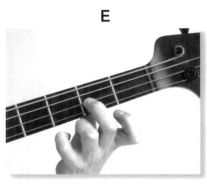

■ To play the note E, place your second finger at the second fret.

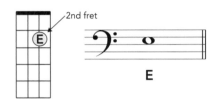

F

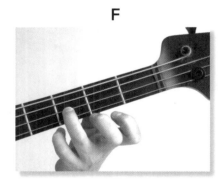

■ To play the note F, place your third finger at the third fret.

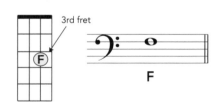

Practice these next exercises several times, slow and easy. Then play them along with the audio. Again, say the note names aloud, or think them, as you play.

Track 15

D-E-F

say or
think : "D   E   F..."

Track 16

Three-Note Groove

► Try to keep your eyes on the page, instead of on your bass.

Now here are some songs to practice *all* the notes you've learned so far on the first and second strings.

Track 17

Two-String Rock

Keep It Clean

To keep your bass lines sounding clean and punchy, try the following:

- If you're plucking the strings with your fingers, let each finger follow through to the next string after it plucks, allowing the lower string to stop your finger's motion. This does two things: 1) it mutes the lower string, keeping it from ringing, and 2) it controls how far your fingers move, increasing your right hand accuracy.

- If you're playing with a pick, allow the side of your thumb to lightly touch any lower strings as you pick; this will mute those strings, preventing them from ringing.

Track 18

That's Right

► Watch that jump from A to E (both played by the second finger). Try to keep it smooth.

Introducing Rests

In addition to notes, songs may also contain silences, or **rests**—beats in which you play nothing at all. A rest is a musical pause. Rests are like notes in that they have their own rhythmic values, instructing you how long (or for how many beats) to pause:

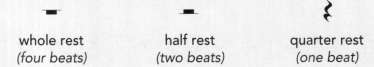

whole rest
(four beats)

half rest
(two beats)

quarter rest
(one beat)

You'll definitely want to stop any previous notes from ringing during a rest. To do this, try the following:

* After an open-string note, like G, touch the string lightly with your left-hand finger(s).

* After a fretted note, like F, decrease the pressure of your left-hand finger on the string.

Track 19

Rest Easy

Track 20

Rock 'n' Rest

Introducing the Pickup

Instead of starting a song with a rest, a **pickup measure** may be used. A pickup measure is an incomplete measure that deletes any opening rests. So, if a pickup has only one beat, you count "1, 2, 3" and start playing on beat 4.

Two New Notes: E♭ and F#

Notice that we skipped the first and fourth frets on the D string? Let's go back and grab 'em.

E♭

▶ Remember: E♭ is one fret *lower* than E. F# is one fret *higher* than F.

■ To play the note E♭, place your first finger at the first fret.

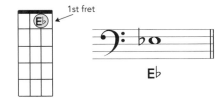

F#

■ To play the note F#, place your fourth finger at the fourth fret.

Now let's try these new notes.

Track 21

E♭-F#

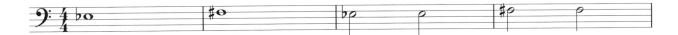

Track 22

My Pickup's Got a Flat!

▶ Notice the pickup measure here. You actually begin playing on beat 4.

Track 23

Mixin' It Up Again

Two-String Review

Here's all the notes we've learned so far, from D to B. That's ten notes in all!

Track 24

Review This!

Track 25

Walk Away

► Use your left-hand technique here (à la page 13).

The Third String: A

Track 26

Are you ready to move ahead? Then it's time for another string. Your new notes, A, B, and C, are all played on the third string.

▶ Notice we're using the same fret positions as on the second string: open, 2nd, and 3rd.

A

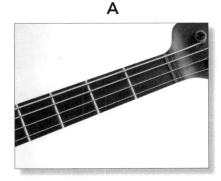

■ To play the note A, pluck the open third string.

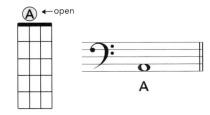

B

■ To play the note B, place your second finger at the second fret.

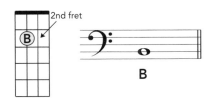

C

■ To play the note C, place your third finger at the third fret.

Track 27

A-B-C

say or think: "A   B   C..."

A-B-C Soup

► Be sure to mute the strings during rests.

Tempo is the speed at which a song is played—from very slow to very fast. For now, try to play at a tempo that allows your eyes to read ahead of the music; this'll give your fingers time to prepare for each note. As you become more confident with the notes, you'll naturally speed up.

Track 29

Brother

Introducing Octaves

If your new A and B sound familiar, they should. They sound much like the A and B on the first string, but they're an "octave" lower. The word *octave* means "eight notes apart." (You'll understand that more a bit later...) Bass players use octaves a lot—the notes of an octave are almost interchangeable, and they can really "fatten up" a bass line—so get used to this new concept.

Track 30

Big Rock

► You can let the strings ring here; octaves sound good that way.

Two New Notes: B♭ and C♯

Did you think we'd skip the first and fourth frets on the A string? Not a chance!

B♭

■ To play the note B♭, place your first finger on the first fret.

B♭

C♯

■ To play the note C♯, place your fourth finger at the fourth fret.

C♯

Now let's put these notes to good use.

Track 31

B♭-C♯

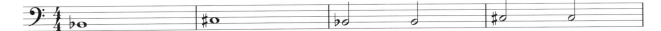

Track 32

Blues Baby!

Introducing Eighth Notes

If you divide a quarter note in half, what you get is an *eighth note*. ♪ ♫
An eighth note looks like a quarter note, but with a flag on it.

Two eighth notes equal one quarter note. To help you keep track of the beat, consecutive eighths are connected with a beam.

To count eighth notes, divide the beat into two, and use "and" between the beats. Practice this, first by counting out loud while tapping your foot on the beat, and then by playing the notes while counting and tapping.

Eighth rests are the same, but you pause instead of playing.

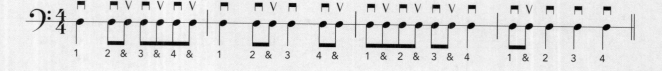

Now, try some songs that use eighth notes. Keep that foot tapping!

Track 33

Eighth-Note Rock

▶ Keep letting your right hand fingers follow through after plucking the strings.

Alternate Picking

If you're using a pick to play these eighth-note lines, try them with *alternate picking*. This is one way to add speed and facility to your bass playing. Alternate picking is a combination of downstrokes (⊓) on the beat (on "1," "2," "3," or "4") and upstrokes (∨) off the beat (on the "ands"). This short exercise on your open A string will give you a better idea of how it's done:

Track 34

Blues By Eight

► Try this song both ways: first with all downstrokes, then with alternate picking.

3/4 Time

The next song is in **3/4** meter. That is, three beats (quarter notes) per measure.

3/4 time feels very different from 4/4 time. Be sure to accent the first beat of each measure, just slightly; this will help you feel the new meter.

Track 35

Amazing Grace

► Notice the pickup measure. The melody begins on beat 3 while the bass rests.

FYI: It's usually the bassist's job to lay down the foundation of a song while other instruments play the melody. The above bass line is a great example of that. (For a real challenge, try singing the melody at the same time that you play your bass part!)

Track 36

Mr. Three

Repeat signs (𝄆   𝄇) tell you to repeat everything in between them. If only one sign appears (𝄇), repeat from the beginning of the piece.

Track 37

Four and Repeat

Track 38

Three and Repeat

► This song has a "new" note, D♯.

D♯ is a really old note with a new name. You already know it as E♭. How can one note have two names? It just depends on which way you approach it, from E or D. Notes like D♯ and E♭ are called **enharmonic equivalents**—a fancy way of saying "two names for the same pitch."

Lesson 5 | The Fourth String: E

The notes E, F, and G are played on the fourth string of the bass. As you practice these new notes, memorize their positions on the staff and ledger lines. You'll definitely use them a lot!

E

■ To play the note E, pluck the open fourth string.

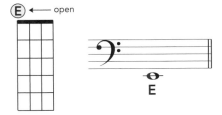

F

■ To play the note F, place your first finger at the first fret.

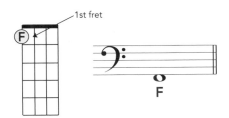

G

■ To play the note G, place your third finger at the third fret.

This is it—the last string!

E-F-G

think: "E   F   G..."

Don't forget to let your eyes read a little ahead while you play.

Fourth-String Strut

Bass Rock

Ties and Dots

The *tie* is a curved line that connects two notes of the same pitch. When you see a tie, play the first note and then hold it for the total value of both notes.

1   2   3   (4   1)   2   3   (4   1   2)   3   4

Ties are useful when you need to extend the value of a note across a bar line.

Another way to extend the value of a note is to use a **dot**. A dot extends any note by one-half its value. Most common is the dotted half note:

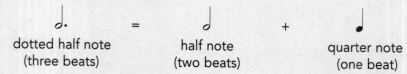

| dotted half note | = | half note | + | quarter note |
| (three beats) | | (two beats) | | (one beat) |

You'll encounter the dotted half note in many songs, especially those that use 3/4 meter.

Track 43

Tongue-Tied

Track 44

Mr. Ballad

► Watch that third-finger jump (from G to C). Make it smooth.

Two More Notes: F♯ and G♯

From the strings that we already know, let's add two more new notes: F♯ and G♯.

F♯

■ To play the note F♯, place your second finger at the second fret.

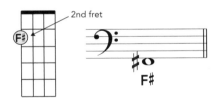

G♯

■ To play the note G♯, place your fourth finger at the fourth fret.

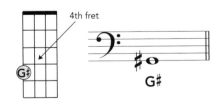

F#-G#

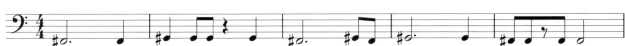

Low Groove

Blues in E

► There's that
D# again!

Steppin' Out

The Dotted Quarter Note

As we know, a dot lengthens a note by one half its time value. When a quarter note is followed by a dot, its time value is increased from 1 beat to 1 1/2 beats.

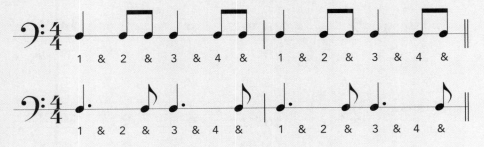

dotted quarter note
(1 1/2 beats)   quarter note
(1 beat)   eighth note
(1/2 beat)

A dotted quarter note is usually followed by an eighth note. This pattern has a total time value of two beats.

To get more comfortable with counting dotted quarter notes, try the following rhythm exercise:

Rockin' Riff

Track 49

▶ The word *riff* is slang for a repeated instrumental figure, or musical idea.

Bossa #1

Track 50

27

Lesson 6 | First Position Review

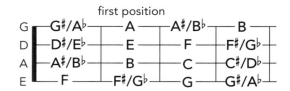

first position

		G#/Ab	A	A#/Bb	B
G		G#/Ab	A	A#/Bb	B
D		D#/Eb	E	F	F#/Gb
A		A#/Bb	B	C	C#/Db
E		F	F#/Gb	G	G#/Ab

We've covered all four strings, but let's double back and review the notes we've learned. This area of the bass neck—from the open strings to fret 4—is called *first position*.

Again, notes that have different names but occupy the same fret (like F♯ and G♭) are referred to as *enharmonic equivalents*. Either note name is acceptable.

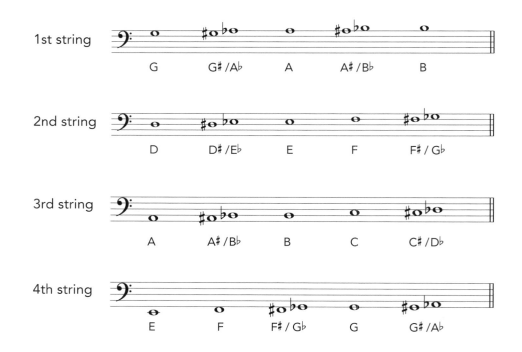

In case you haven't noticed, when we play in first position, each finger gets assigned to one fret—first finger to the first fret, second finger to the second fret, third finger to the third fret, and fourth finger to the fourth fret. This is called the *one-finger-per-fret* rule. This way, we can easily cover all the notes in first position without having to shift hand position, and we always know how to finger each note.

One-Finger-Per Fret Rock

Track 53

New Flats

Staccato

If you see a dot (•) above or below a note, it means to play the note short, a.k.a. *staccato*. To do this, release pressure on the note with your left-hand finger, or mute the note if it's an open string.

Track 54

Funky

staccato

Track 55

Punky

More Octaves

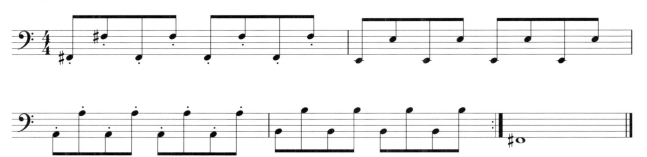

Technique

We'll take a look at our left and right hands again.

The Left Hand

Try this exercise. Remember to keep your fingers down as you play each note.

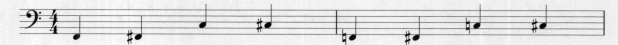

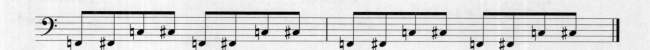

The Right Hand

Now we will practice skipping strings. Notice that every other measure is played staccato. Pay close attention to your right hand to keep the strings from ringing. Go very slowly!

Track 58

Mr. Technique

2/2 Time

In *2/2 time*, there are two beats per measure, and the half note gets the beat. This actually feels a lot like 4/4, but you only tap your foot twice in each measure.

Track 59

Two for Espresso

Track 60

Hail to the Bassist

Notes at the Fifth Fret

Track 61

Before we move on to some new topics, let's grab a few more notes up higher on the fretboard. These are all found at the fifth fret and should be played with your fourth (pinky) finger.

A

■ To play the note A, place your fourth finger at the fifth fret of the *fourth* string.

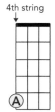
4th string

A

D

■ To play the note D, place your fourth finger at the fifth fret of the *third* string.

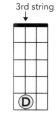
3rd string

D

G

■ To play the note G, place your fourth finger at the fifth fret of the *second* string.

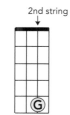
2nd string

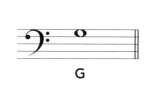
G

C

■ To play the note C, place your fourth finger at the fifth fret of the *first* string.

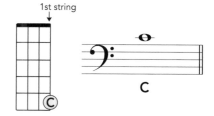
1st string

C

You'll probably want to move your hand up the fretboard, just a bit, to reach that fifth fret...

Introducing Second Position

It's easier to play notes at the fifth fret if you move your hand up the neck to *second position*. In second position, your first finger moves up to the *second fret*. The rest of your fingers fall into place on the adjacent frets (following the one-finger-per-fret rule).

Track 62

► Play this in second position, using just your pinky.

Fifth-Fret Warrior

Of course, the new note here is the high C, so let's take advantage of it.

Track 63

Hittin' the High C

There's More Than One Place To Find a Note!

The more you play bass, the more you'll discover there's more than one place to find the same note. For instance, we now have two places to play the notes A, D, and G.

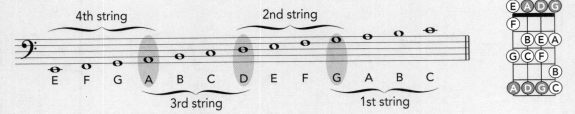

Which fingering you choose depends on:

- *Where your fingers are.* Are you in first position? Second position?
- *What sound you prefer.* Open strings have a different sound than fretted notes.

Introducing Tablature or "Tab"

From now on, we'll be seeing a new type of musical notation called **tablature**, or **"tab"** for short. It consists of four lines, one for each string of your bass. The numbers written on the lines indicate which fret to play in order to sound the correct notes.

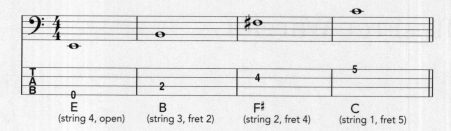

Tab is a very popular notation method for bass music and can be used to show finger patterns and positions on the neck. Refer to it when you need clarification on where to play a note. Otherwise, keep reading the notes on the staff.

Track 64

Tab This!

► This song plays well in second position. (Notice the tab.)

Track 65

Tab That!

► Try this riff in first position, then in second, as indicated.

Lesson 8 | Major Scales

Now that you've got a handle on all four strings up to the fifth fret, it's time to start learning about scales. "What's a scale?" you ask. A *scale* is an arrangement of notes in a specific, sequential pattern. Most scales use eight notes, with the top and bottom notes being an octave apart.

Two things give a scale its name: its lowest note (called the *root*) and the pattern of whole and half steps it uses. A *major* scale is always built using this interval formula:

whole – whole – half – whole – whole – whole – half

Remember: On the bass, a whole step is two frets, a half step is one fret. Let's take a look!

Track 66

▶ Notice that in an E major scale, there are four sharps: F#, G#, C#, and D#.

E Major

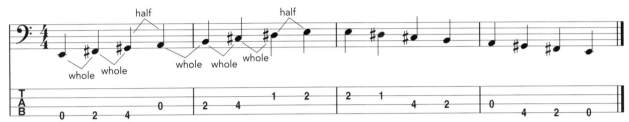

Track 67

▶ Notice that in an F major scale, there is one flat: B♭.

F Major

Track 68

▶ Notice that in a G major scale, there is one sharp: F#.

G Major

Key Signatures

In written music, a *key signature* is found at the beginning of the staff, between the clef and the time signature. It defines what notes will be sharp or flat—or essentially, what key you'll be playing in.

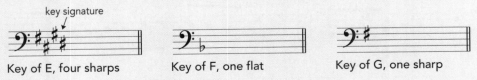

Key of E, four sharps   Key of F, one flat   Key of G, one sharp

So What's a Key?

Good question. Key and scale are almost the same thing. When we know a scale—like E major—we have all the notes we need to play in the corresponding key—like E major!

Like scales, keys have two components:

- a root, or **tonic**, which is the defining note. This is often (but not always) the first or last note in a piece of music, and it usually feels the most resolved, or "at rest."

- a **quality**. In this case, major.

Just remember, to play in a key, use the notes of the scale with the same name. For example, to play in the key of E major, use the notes of an E major scale. To play in G major, use the notes of a G major scale.

Track 69

E Jam

► Watch the key signature. It tells you what notes to play sharp (or flat) in the music.

Track 70

Unplugged in G

Track 71

Descent in F

36

Track 72

Name That Key!

More Major Scales

Now, we'll take a look at some more major scales! Notice that major scales (and keys) contain either sharps *or* flats—but never both.

Track 73

A Major

▶ A major has three sharps: C♯, F♯, and G♯.

Track 74

B♭ Major

▶ B♭ major has two flats: B♭ and E♭.

Here is a good one for second position.

Track 75

C Major

▶ C major is a popular scale—it has no sharps or flats.

37

Minor Scales

Since we just learned six major scales, let's even things out by learning some *minor* scales. A minor scale is built like this:

whole – half – whole – whole – half – whole – whole

Wow, what was that? Let's take a closer look!

Track 76

E Minor

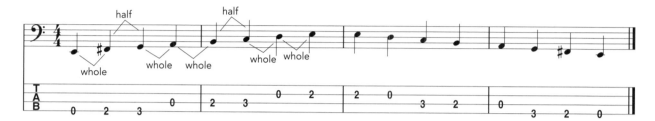

Track 77

F Minor

Track 78

G Minor

Major vs. Minor

The difference between major and minor scales is not just about whole and half steps—it's about how they **sound.** Take a minute to compare a major and a minor scale—like G major and G minor. Notice how each makes you feel? It's difficult to put into words, but generally we say that major scales (and keys) have a strong, upbeat, or happy quality, while minor scales and keys have a darker, sadder quality.

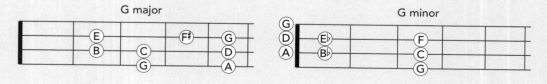

Minor scales have key signatures, too. But we'll explore those in Level 2. For now, let's try some songs in minor keys.

Rage in E Minor

Sad Story

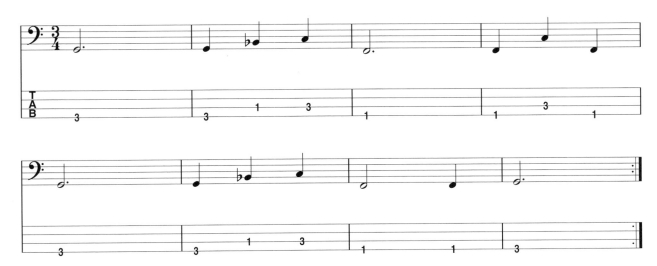

Why?

Hammer-Ons and Pull-Offs

The hammer-on and pull-off are great techniques for building speed and improving your left hand coordination—and they sound cool.

1. To play a **hammer-on**, place your first finger on the B♭ shown. Pluck the note, and then "hammer down" with your third finger onto the second note, C. The force of that finger fretting the string causes the note to sound (without plucking).

2. To play a **pull-off**, start with both fingers planted on their notes. Pluck the note C, then "pull off" with your third finger, letting the note B♭ sound. Got it?

Hammer Head

► Use your first and third fingers for this. Then try your second and fourth fingers.

Pull My Finger!

Combo Platter

More Minor Scales

Let's add some more minor scales to our vocabulary.

Track 85

A Minor

► A minor has no sharps or flats—like C major!

Track 86

B♭ Minor

Track 87

C Minor

► This one requires a bit of a stretch on the top string.

Name That Key, Pt. 2

Is it major or is it minor? Listen for the quality, and find the tonic note.

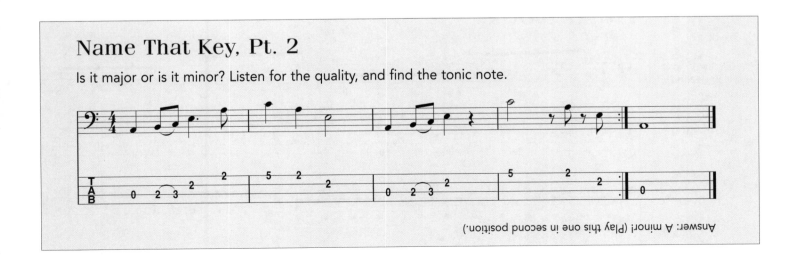

Answer: A minor! (Play this one in second position.)

Lesson 10 Style

Finally, let's put to use all that we've learned. In this lesson, we will play through some common styles of music. Roll up your sleeves, and let's go!

Track 88

'50s Rock

Track 89

► This one plays well in second position.

Hard Rock

42

Alternative Rock

Track 91

Rap Metal

Pop Rock

Pop Ballad

R&B

▶ This song uses a multi-measure rest. The bass waits four measures, then begins playing.

Reggae

► Play this one in second position—you'll have to stretch to reach the low F.

Funk

Jazz

Bossa #2

Country

► This one requires a position shift. Also, to play the same fret on adjacent strings, try "rolling" your finger across.

Review & More

Notes on Frets 1-5

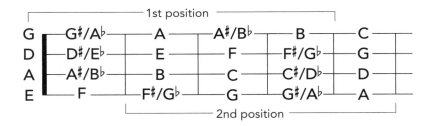

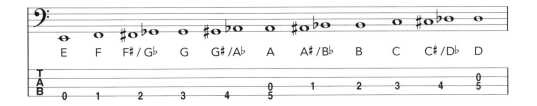

Movable Scale Forms

In case you haven't noticed, the neck of the bass is very geometric; patterns and shapes are consistent. The following major and minor scale patterns can be used all over the neck. Just find the desired root note on strings 3 or 4 (see diagram at right), then apply the pattern of your choice—and there's your scale. We'll explore this further in Level 2.

Major

Minor

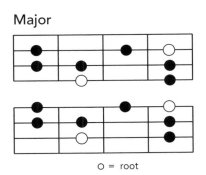

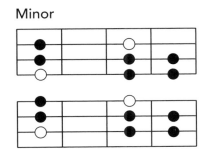

O = root

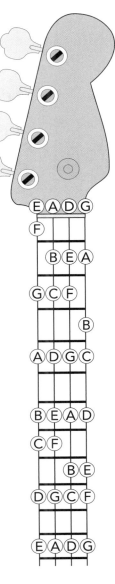

How to Change a String

If you're missing a string or your strings are old and need replacing, you'll need to know how to change them. The diagram below should help. Once you've inserted the ball-end of a string at the bridge, you need to wrap the other end around the tuning peg at the headstock. To do this, first insert the string in the posthole. Then, bend it sharply to hold it in place, and begin winding. You should allow enough slack to wrap the string around the peg 3 to 4 times; any excess can be removed with a good wire cutter.

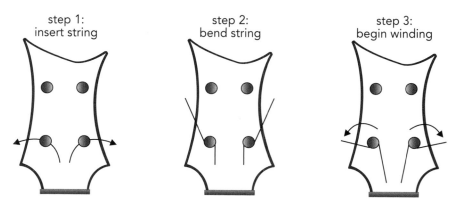

step 1:
insert string

step 2:
bend string

step 3:
begin winding

Keep in mind, new strings need to be stretched before you can expect them to hold their pitch. You can do this by playing on them awhile and tuning them up several times until each string remains in tune. (Lightly pulling on the strings one at a time, initially, can also help stretch them out.)

Adjusting the Bridge

String height (or "action") can be adjusted by raising or lowering the bridge saddles of your bass. Some saddles require a small screwdriver, but most use a small Allen wrench, which can be purchased at a hardware store if one did not come with your bass at the time of purchase.

The Truss Rod

Remember: your bass is wood (unless you purchased a graphite-neck model). With the changes of season come changes in your bass neck. Most basses have a steel rod through the neck, which can be adjusted to tighten or loosen neck tension. If you notice buzzing to be more frequent, it is a good idea to take your bass in to get the neck adjusted. If possible, watch how a professional does it so you can learn how to adjust the truss rod yourself.